The Xenophobe's Guide to The Icelanders

Richard Sale

RAVETTE BOOKS

Published by Ravette Books Ltd.
Egmont House
8 Clifford Street
London W1X 1RB
Tel & Fax (01 0403) 711443

Editor – Catriona Tulloch Scott
Series Editor – Anne Tauté

Cover design – Jim Wire
Printer – Cox & Wyman Ltd.
Production – Oval Projects Ltd.

An Oval Project
Produced for Ravette Books,
an Egmont Company.

Acknowledgement and grateful thanks
are given to:

Forest Books for permission to use the
extract from 'The eagle flies over' by
Matthias Johannessen, translated by
Marshall Brement, from the collection
of his verse, *The Naked Machine*, 1988.

William Jón Holm for his poem, The
Icelandic Language, also published in a
different translation in *The Dead Get
By With Everything* by Milkwood
Editions (USA), 1990.

Contents

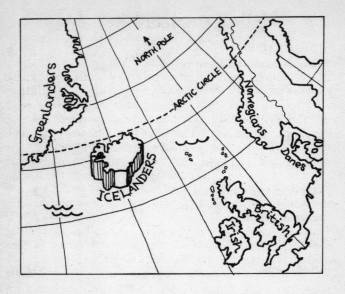

There are 260,000 Icelanders, of whom 140,000 live in Reykjavik and its satellite villages. In all its recorded history a total of no more than 1 million people have ever lived in Iceland.

Nationalism and Identity

Forewarned

The Icelanders are Europeans, but only up to a point, the point lying about 200 miles offshore. They would like to join the European Union, feeling that they have a huge contribution to make. But there are difficulties. For one thing, any nation that thinks it is the greatest on earth would have problems joining a club which includes the French. It is also difficult for the Icelanders to accept that they would not have the same voting power as the British and the Germans. When it is pointed out that there are very few of them in comparison, they do not understand. One country, one vote, surely?

But the Icelanders' real problem is fishing. Cod is the basis of their economy and they are nervous of foreign trawlers ruining their livelihood. One of the reasons they like the British is because they lost the last Cod War. It was a friendly war and the Icelanders like losers, as long as they lose to Iceland that is.

The idea of being different makes the Icelanders proud of their country. Nowhere else are there lava deserts, active volcanoes and icecaps. At the same time they recognise that as a nation they are tiny and of limited standing in the world. The insecurity this creates makes the Icelanders, a very close-knit nation with a developed sense of community, behave as though they were indeed the centre of the universe.

It was recently discovered that in the winter of 1002/1003 Snorri Thorfinnsson was born in Vinland (Newfoundland), the first non-Indian American. It is only a matter of time before the Icelanders file a lawsuit claiming North America on behalf of Snorri's surviving relatives.

How They See Themselves

A few years ago the Icelandic system suffered a shock when blood-typing suggested that the Icelanders might be of Celtic, rather than Viking, stock. To have the same roots as the Americans (who are basically Irish and therefore quite beyond the pale) and even to share characteristics with the English (who are amiable enough but arrogant) was almost more than could be tolerated. Thankfully the results turned out to be wrong and perhaps, even better, to suggest that the Vikings kidnapped a few Celtic women on the way. The national psyche was restored to health.

Icelanders hold themselves in the very highest esteem. They are the sons of Vikings, the greatest of all ancient races, renowned for their strength, fortitude, good looks and masculine values. The fact that the Vikings are also famous for rape and pillage is quietly ignored, as is their somewhat dubious attitude towards women. Icelanders are also reluctant to talk about Ingolf, the Viking who found Iceland. As a mark of respect they have named the spot where he landed Ingolfshofδi, but they put it in small print on their maps so that as few people as possible notice that it is merely a knob of rock some three miles out to sea.

As proof of their innate superiority the Icelanders point out that Iceland is the navel of the world. If you doubt the veracity of this claim you need only consult the Viking Sagas, the greatest of all literary achievements, where this view is expressed countless times during the course of long meandering tales of murder and revenge.

Icelanders believe themselves to be the best of people living in the best of countries. They point out that they have the biggest and best of many things. They have the largest glacier in Europe, making France's Mer de Glace look like an ice cube by comparison. Their waterfalls are higher, more powerful and more beautiful than any others in Europe. And even if Strokkur, the only surviving geyser, is smaller than the one in America's Yellowstone National Park, they point out that it can be found at Geysir, the Icelandic name now used to describe all such natural gushing phenomena.

The island also has the most westerly point in Europe, a fact guaranteed to annoy the Irish who have erected numerous signs in Dingle claiming the same thing.

Icelanders see themselves as cultured and sophisticated, and are very proud of their artistic heritage and desire for independence. These points are always included in speeches by Vigdis Finnbogadóttir, Iceland's woman President, whose comments are quoted as gospel and prefaced with a friendly "As President Vigdis says...". In fact, so often is this phrase used that it has become a kind of valediction.

How They See Others

It might be imagined that the Icelanders, sharing a mutual Viking heritage with the Scandinavian nations, would see them as brothers. Not so.

The Norwegians are laughed at for their enthusiasm for outdoor pursuits which is looked on as proof of what the Icelanders thought anyway, that the Norwegians are slow-witted and dull. Ask the Icelanders about the paintings of Munch, the music of Grieg and the books of Hamsun and they will point out that it is likely that those individuals were descended from Icelandic Vikings who went home for the weekend and were stranded by a recalcitrant tide or wind. The discovery of North Sea oil and the fact that it has made the Norwegians very rich has led to a change of view. Now the Norwegians are seen as slow-witted, dull, and quite disgustingly lucky.

The Swedes are considered to be self-centred, sex-mad and too frequently given to bouts of pleasure seeking – a clear case of the blond pot speaking unkindly of the blond kettle.

Norwegians and Swedes are also resented for being Arctic nations. With its name and its wild landscape Iceland might be expected to lie within the Arctic Circle, but only the island of Grimsey off the northern coast manages to do so, and then only by a few yards. As a consequence Icelanders deride the Circle, and say that only one man in Iceland can be bothered to cross it. He is the vicar of Grimsey and he only does so because the Circle runs through the centre of his bed.

The existence of an American air-force base in Iceland means that it is flooded with American television programmes and almost the entire population speaks English. Ironically, despite the impetus to learn English provided by the Americans, they are not much liked. The Icelanders are proud of the fact that it was one of their men, Leif Erikkson, who discovered the New World (several centuries before that upstart Columbus) although they now wish he hadn't. They like American dollars, but resent the servicemen who spend them. They tune in all day to American television but constantly moan about its poor quality and the effect it is having on the younger generation.

To get their own back, they banished the Americans to an inhospitable, lonely corner of the island on the pretext that Iceland's only international airport (Keflavik) is there. Oddly, if you ask, they will also claim that Keflavik lies in this wilderness because it was built close to where the Americans were.

Special Relationships

The Icelanders have a special relationship with the Danes but this has nothing to do with their common Viking origin. Until early this century Denmark ruled Iceland and this has spoilt a relationship that might have been built on the mutual mistrust of family members. Older Icelanders have a saying that Danes make good rulers for Danes, which is a roundabout way of saying that they should stay at home with their Lego. Younger Icelanders are inclined to a different view and are busy re-writing history. As Danish is still the first foreign language taught in Icelandic schools (though it is increasingly being replaced by English) young Icelanders develop an affinity with the Danes. They see them as cousins and can be wildly enthusiastic about them – as long as there are no Danes actually present.

The English have a special place in the Icelandic heart, having lost the Cod Wars. They are looked on as laughable and lovable eccentrics, much given to coming second. The Icelanders find this latter characteristic hilarious and strangely reassuring.

Icelanders share with the Luxembourgers an inferiority complex born of being so few in number. Luxembourg has the largest community of Icelandic ex-patriots in Europe since the European headquarters of Icelandair is situated there. (Icelandair operates nearly all the flights to the island, the normal shared ownership of routes not applying as no-one else flies there, except the Scandinavians' SAS company, which just goes to show that you can't even trust your cousins.) The Icelanders and Luxembourgers both score no points in the Eurovision Song Contest and regularly lose at football.

As many as 10,000 Icelanders emigrated to Canada in the 1880s and ties have been maintained. When an

Icelander meets a Canadian, the Canadian is expected to know the relatives of the Icelander he is speaking to.

The Russians are special for different reasons. Russian trawlers regularly dock and disgorge men of seemingly overwhelming stupidity who can be persuaded to exchange much-prized bottles of fierce vodka for clapped-out Ladas and other cars. Those who taste the vodka have no doubts about who has the better deal.

How They Would Like Others to See Them

Iceland is a large, almost uninhabited country. The population is about the same as that of Leicester, though the infrastructure is more like that of Los Angeles. To go with the latter, the Icelanders have the aspirations of the residents of Hollywood, even if it is fish that must pay for everything.

As proof of their sophistication, Icelanders point to the publication of a monthly English-language newspaper. How many other countries produce a paper in a language other than their own? Its writers even use colloquialisms to prove their grasp of English. The paper is indeed impressive; however, the mix of cliché and dated slang makes it quite clear that it has not been written by someone whose first language is English.

Character

Iceland came very quickly into the 20th century. Having been an isolated, insular race until 1940, the Icelanders suddenly found themselves the centre of attention. Invaded (for their own good, or so they were told) by the British and Americans, they discovered in 1945 that they were rich beyond their wildest dreams. New markets for their fish made them for many years the wealthiest nation in Europe. But this happened to a simple country people, and rustic attitudes live on.

The average farmer is considered well able to solve most of life's problems given twenty minutes, a hammer and a piece of string. This prejudice (and the Icelanders have never let a few facts get in the way of a good prejudice) was reinforced by the country's early roadbuilders who were book-trained engineers and quite useless. Even their first successes, the bridges they built to connect outlying parts of the country to the main roads, became an object of scorn: the folk they were built to serve used them in order to migrate to the towns, and the bridges fell into disrepair and disuse behind them.

Being new to the concept of town-dwelling, the Icelanders still find its rules difficult. If you have been used to riding into the nearest village and hitching your horse to a rail outside the shop you want to visit, you expect to do the same with your car. There is an underground car park in Reykjavik. It is empty. The streets, by contrast, are filled with apparently abandoned cars. Parking meters and restrictions have been introduced. They are ignored.

If you are driving through town and see someone you know on the pavement or in a car coming the other way, you will stop for a chat, just as you would if you met him on horseback. Such conversations last as long as they last. If that is a very long time, and it often is, the queue of vehicles behind the talkers will soon be miles long.

The Icelanders tolerate this behaviour up to a point, though foreigners find it hard to fathom. Those who become sufficiently irate might blow their horns. If you do this, the offending motorists, and everyone else within earshot, will fix you with a withering stare. However, there is an up-side. If you are crossing a road, particularly if you are loaded with parcels, drivers will stop for you. Probably.

People are always on the move, dropping the children off, going shopping, picking the children up again, going swimming. Reykjavik appears to have twice the number of vehicles that a city its size would normally have as Icelanders do everything by car.

The Essential Icelander

An Icelander has held the title of the World's Strongest Man and there have been two Icelandic Miss Worlds. There has also been a surprising number of chess grand-masters for such a small country. These facts reinforce the Icelanders' belief that they are a nation of strong, beautiful and intelligent people. To these attributes could be added the term grim-faced. Look at any group or group photo of Icelanders and one would imagine they are attending a funeral or the execution of a mutual friend.

The Icelanders are remarkably honest. It is impossible for an Icelander to deceive someone he knows, or confronts face to face, though there have been some notable swindles by post. Honesty is part of the national character to such an extent that when an Icelander passed himself off as an Irishman so that he could compete in the world handball championships, it made headline news. (So bad at the deception was he that he was quickly discovered and banned from competition for life.)

The Icelander is very individualistic, but he is also addicted to clubs and groups, the more frivolous the better. Try the club for 'People Who Have Been Insulted By Politicians' for a start. This enthusiasm for clubs does not extend as far as the joining of trades unions. The Icelander finds such organisations altogether too earnest.

Beliefs and Values

Elves, Trolls and Dwarfes

Although it is not obvious to every visitor to the island, Iceland is inhabited by a whole host of folk besides the Icelanders. There are elves, about the size of ordinary people but who mostly stay hidden from view. They live in hills. There are trolls. Unlike Norwegian trolls, the Icelandic troll is not small and ugly and does not live under a bridge in mortal fear of billy goats. Icelandic trolls are ten to twelve feet tall and live in mountains. And there are dwarfs. Icelandic dwarfs are as tiny as might be expected and live in rocks.

The living quarters of this army of hidden folk (known in Icelandic as *smáfolk* – small folk, an odd name when applied to twelve-feet-tall trolls) are easy to spot: they are the particularly beautiful rocks, hills and mountains.

The visitor who thinks that all this is nonsense under-estimates the hold the tales of hidden folk have on the Icelandic mind. The main road from Reykjavik to Selfoss bears left for no good reason a few miles beyond Hveragerði, near a church on the right. It does this in order to avoid an elf hill. Even today, town streets are aligned to avoid elf hills and dwarf rocks. Past experience has taught the Icelanders that to attempt to build over a smáfolk site is useless. Bulldozers will fail, hammers will break, nothing can be done to destroy the site, so you might just as well go round it.

Young people are brought up on stories of the small folk which suggests that the old pagan Viking roots are closer to the surface than many Icelanders would care to admit. A grandmother will have told of the time her sheep went missing for a few days and an elf woman came to apologise, saying she had needed ewe's milk for her sick infant and telling her where the sheep could be found.

At a recent public lecture on the small folk, when the speaker asked how many of the audience believed in elves, about 80% of those present raised their hands. Of them 50% had spoken to an elf and 25% had seen one. One man admitted to having made love to an elf (*alfur* in Icelandic) but it turned out he was hard of hearing and had thought the speaker had been speaking about a cow (*calfur*).

An Icelander living in Canada placed an advertisement in the national Icelandic newspaper. He wanted a female elf to go to Canada as companion to a male elf who had inadvertently travelled with a group of emigrating Icelanders. The male elf, starved of love and friendship, was making a nuisance of himself. The paper followed the story up, hoping to join in the joke, but the advertiser was not joking which probably came as no surprise to the readers.

If you ask Icelanders about the hidden folk you will be told a story about Niels Bohr, the Danish physicist.

Iceland feels a kinship with this Nobel prizewinner as the country was under Danish rule when he was at the peak of his powers. He used to have a lucky horseshoe hanging in his study. An incredulous visitor said that he found it hard to believe that so eminent a scientist could believe in such things. "Oh I don't," said Bohr, "but I'm told it works even if you don't believe in it."

Class and Wealth

The ancient kings of Iceland being Danish, there is no Icelandic aristocracy. In its absence, and since the Icelanders have realised that there are no classless societies in Europe, several 'classes' are developing.

One of the more interesting is a class based on family history. Few families can trace their families back more than a few generations, but that has not stopped a thriving trade in the creation of family trees going back to the inhabitants of the first longboats to have been drawn up on the southern beaches. This has led to a corresponding increase in interest in the Vikings, and a book has been published on their sayings. It is a surprisingly fat book in view of the fact that history suggests they only used two phrases, i.e. "take that" (to a man), and (to a woman) "take this".

Another class is education-based, and 'ill-educated' is an increasingly derogatory term. This is odd because the Icelanders have an abiding suspicion of education. Useful subjects in particular, such as science, engineering and languages, are not deemed to be worth studying. On the other hand, the Icelanders are impressed by lawyers and doctors, and are also very fond of philosophers. A poor philosopher stands higher on the social scale than an engineer or a good plumber, with the result that on occasions neither Icelandic theories nor Icelandic pipes hold water.

The most significant class is based on money. In this the Icelanders are no different from other European countries, though enthusiasm for believing that the rich are a better class is taken to extremes. They must be better – they have a house abroad and a big car.

The Icelander is impressed by others' wealth, but jealous of it. Any show of wealth is met by a public sneer, implying he dislikes ostentation, but a private grinding of teeth. In Iceland it is best to make your money quickly, before anyone knows about it. Money, or the lack of it in comparison to others, causes great stress, and it is surprising that life expectancy is still rising, rather than falling like a stone.

An illustration of the Icelandic attitude to social standing is a story of some fishermen making their way down to a quay very early one morning on their way to a day's fishing. They passed a house and as they did so the door opened and out came a group of professional men. A merchant and a doctor, both unsteady on their feet, were carrying the drunken form of the local mayor while a clergyman carried the mayor's hat. Seeing the fishermen, the group looked away, not because they were ashamed but because in Icelandic society the professionals were of a higher standing and would not dream of talking to rough fishing types. This story fits in neatly with the Icelandic view that those at the top of the social pile, while enviably rich, are either drunkards or mad.

Style

The Icelanders have style.

They suffer a climate that is best described as miserable but do not allow it to get in the way of wearing the trendiest garb. If this decrees open-toed sandals, then these will be worn, even if the snow is four feet deep.

Style is learned early. Stand outside any school and you will be treated to a show of the latest in world fashion. Even the Icelandic horse gets in on the act, having five gaits rather than the four favoured by the rest of the world's horses.

The Icelanders are among the most house-proud people on earth. They have all the latest gadgets and gizmos, though this has as much to do with keeping up with the Magnussons as it has with style. If a new television model comes on to the market it has to be purchased and the old one put in the bedroom, guest room or kitchen. This overt materialism means that most Icelanders would almost prefer to live in a cardboard box than do without the latest hi-fi or electronic aid. But the box would be furnished and equipped to the highest standards.

In contrast to the style of their interiors, the electrics and plumbing of most Icelandic houses are a mess. Even the best-appointed houses will have a light fitting hanging off the ceiling and a leaking tap.

The Icelanders' enthusiasm for interiors is not translated to the outside. The climate is harsh. Plants die quickly unless they are lovingly cared for, in which case they die slowly. Gardening has not caught on, which means that the only fad not to have been imported from Europe or America is for garden centres. The climate also destroys any attempt to keep the outside of buildings tidy, so that even the smartest hotels have concrete exteriors, the concrete blotched like a modern art painting. (Scaffolding,

17

which curiously for a country that has no trees to speak of is wooden, is attached to buildings by bits and pieces of string and old electrical flex.)

The buildings are roofed with corrugated iron which is regularly painted to keep it rust and leak free. Bright colours are cheaper than pastel ones so the cheapest and brightest are used. The towns and villages look as though they have been built by primary school children.

Style is expensive, but since it is essential to his way of life, the Icelander lives on credit cards and borrowed money. Next to his car and his electronic gadgetry, his credit rating is the closest thing to an Icelander's heart. Credit cards are accepted in all hotels and shops, down to the smallest kiosk. Indeed, if you offer a shop assistant cash for even a tube of toothpaste, it will be assumed that you have no credit rating at all. You will be pointed out to other assistants and followed about in case you do a bit of shoplifting.

Green Issues

Having the last great wilderness in Europe, you would expect the Icelanders to be a green nation. This is not the case, at least not if green issues stand in the way of profit.

The Icelanders have an ambivalent attitude towards nature. There are many National Parks set up to protect the best of the landscape, but a bounty is paid for shooting Arctic foxes, and there is an ongoing debate over the rights and wrongs of whaling.

When the earliest Viking settlers arrived in Iceland there were forests where now there are just mossy deserts. The Vikings cut down the trees for their long boats and soon there were no trees to speak of. Today, those who wish to can visit the National Forest which lies just outside the northern town of Akureyri. The humorously-inclined visitor could count the trees – it wouldn't take long – though it would not be advisable to tell a local the number, for at such times the Icelandic sense of humour could shrivel and die.

This is ironical because the Icelanders still laugh when recalling that one of the ways in which American soldiers, for whom Iceland was an unpopular posting, were encouraged to come to the island was to be told that there was a beautiful, blonde virgin beneath every tree.

With the increasing importance of tourism to the economy there is definitely a colour shift towards green. It is, after all, the colour of the American dollar.

Religion

Like most nationalities the Icelanders are very religious in a crisis. Otherwise they are one of the least religious societies in Europe. The fatalism that was bred of fishing and a harsh climate led them in the past to attribute sufferings to God's will. Today God has been removed from the equation, but similar reasoning allows the Icelander to assume that everyone's problems are their own fault. Except for his own, of course.

The Eurovision Song Contest

In the rest of Europe the Eurovision Song Contest is seen as at best a joke, at worst a bad joke. For years the Icelanders watched the Contest with a mixture of envy and scorn. They wanted to be allowed to compete but recognised that their songs were so superior they were bound to win.

Knowing this to be true the organisers would not allow them to compete, and only after years of trying were they finally allowed to enter.

They were convinced they would win. The newspapers talked of a walkover and on the night of the Contest the streets were empty, the entire population having gone indoors to watch the inevitable victory. Their defeat was a culture shock, one that they took several years (and much talk of conspiracy) to get over.

They now have the same opinion of the Contest as the rest of Europe and even express a fear of winning, since the Icelandic economy, which is in a fragile state, could not survive having to stage the next event. Indeed, if it wasn't for the fact that the Norwegians appear to have a monopoly on last place, the Icelanders would favour the view that the Contest is so ludicrous that coming last was the only sensible course.

Behaviour

Family

The Icelanders have a strong sense of family. Children help with the chores and, despite increased affluence and satellite television, there is a marked absence of the conflict that affects other Europeans. Perhaps this is because family life is less frantic. The children only work at school from 9 a.m. until 1 p.m. (or sometimes 2 p.m.), so there is more time for their social lives.

Until a few years ago it was quite usual for parents to move in with their children when old age made life difficult for them. A common story was of fathers turning up on the doorsteps of daughters a day or two after the funeral of the mother. "Well," they would say, "here I am, where do you want me to sleep?" The trend is now away from this, with old folk going into purpose-built homes.

Feminism

Icelandic women are strong-willed and independent, both qualities dating from the fishing tradition, when the women stayed at home, organised the farm, and did everything while waiting for their men to return; often they did not.

Since they have maintained their strength and independence, feminism is seen as a backward step, for why accept equality when you have superiority? It is somewhat surprising that the modern Icelandic woman marries the modern Icelandic man.

The only battleground of the sexes is politics where strong-minded women have suffered at the hands of weak-minded men for years. To counteract this a party called the Women's List has been formed, which is dedicated to establishing a government of national strength. Whether it succeeds, and whether it yields national unity as well, remains to be seen. Ask any Icelandic man and he will tell you that as far as he is concerned it can remain to be seen for ever.

Fishing communities have always had a high number of single mothers because of the limited life expectancy of fishermen. There appear to be even more single mothers today, for Iceland has the highest illegitimate birthrate in Europe. As there is no social stigma attached to being an unmarried mother, it is no longer considered necessary to drown the father of your child.

21

Sex

It is claimed that where foreign trawlers docked in Iceland many years ago there are now quite a few dark-haired, dark-eyed children. One place in the eastern fjords was even euphemistically called Congo as a result. This suggests that the Icelandic attitude to sex was always fairly liberal, sex being seen as a fun activity to be indulged in often, rather than something to do with the lights off. Things haven't changed.

Liberal attitudes mean that the Icelandic man has never bothered to develop a series of 'chat up' lines. A straightforward 'yes' or 'no' is all the conversation which occurs before the action starts. One result of this is that Icelandic women like foreign males who spend half the night 'chatting them up' before moving on to the main event.

Animals

Some years ago the Icelanders made news by banning dogs from their towns. They told the world that the ban was due to problems with dog mess and the worms it carried. But the real reason was that the Reykjavik authorities thought that dog-owning reeked too much of the rural past. The sophisticated town dweller, it was proposed, didn't need a sheep dog. Dog-owning is now allowed again, though the cost of the dog licence is extortionate to reinforce official disapproval.

The story is told of a tourist fishing in a river in the Icelandic heartland. He was appalled that his Icelandic companions kept every fish they caught. His attitude was the European one of fishing for sport. The Icelanders did not understand this concept. Fish are for eating: if you go fishing the idea is to catch free food.

Shopping

A first-time visitor to Iceland could be forgiven for believing that every shop assistant in the land is called Hilda, for that, apparently, is what every Icelander calls out when he is in a shop. In fact, he is shouting 'herδu' which means 'here', or 'me next'. Shopping involves selecting your item and then pushing and shoving your way to the front of the throng at the counter, all the while shouting 'herδu'. To an Icelander the idea of queueing, let alone the queue itself, is inconceivable, and he is seen at his worst in the state alcohol shops, especially on a Friday night.

The first supermarkets to be built in Iceland imported the traditional European check-out system, but with the corridors to the check-out tills being made a little longer to stop the fighting. Now, many years later, the Icelander does wait in sullen line, but if there is the slightest chance of being able to sneak forward, then be assured, he will.

On Saturday mornings there is a market in Reykjavik's main underground car park. Stalls sell everything from motor bike bits to washing machines and the latest PCs, though junk and secondhand CDs are the most popular items. Icelanders flock to this market, not just for the bargains on offer but for the opportunity it gives them to ignore queues, to barge and shout, and generally to misbehave. It also allows them to finger the goods on offer, something they seem strangely addicted to.

The shops open at 10 a.m. Visitors who arrive in Iceland on a Friday evening assume this is because Friday night does not finish until 9 a.m. on Saturday. In fact, the shops open at 10 a.m. every day.

Conversation and Gestures

A famous Icelandic poet used four-line verses to insult his contemporaries. The short verses were humorous, but cutting. In doing this the poet was not creating something new, but reinforcing a tradition that was centuries old. Even today there are gatherings where everybody has to invent and speak a four-line verse that humorously insults one or more of his fellow guests.

The essence of Icelandic conversation is the insult. Icelanders are born with a talent for it and use it fluidly from an early age. Because of their farming and fishing ancestry the most telling jibes involve sheep and fish. It is a very serious matter to refer to an Icelander as a sheep or a codhead, and an ability to run very fast while panic-stricken is the only possible defence if sufficient umbrage is taken. (It is interesting to note that the Icelander is more likely to be offended by a suggestion that he is a sheep than that his father had a marked preference for ewes over women.) Equally potent is the suggestion that the Icelander is lazy, stupid or uncultured. All these might be true, though laziness is far from being a national characteristic, but that is not the point.

In conversation the Icelanders are wonderfully free of the English habit of saying everything other than what is actually meant. Once a subject has been brought up for discussion, all aspects of it can be thoroughly and honestly explored. This does not mean that all topics of conversation are allowed. Never ask how much an Icelander earns, and do not under any circumstances criticise his driving.

Despite the long tradition of swopping insults, there has never been an Icelandic tradition of gestures, rude or otherwise. So they import them. For instance, they have adopted the German one of tapping the side of the forehead to indicate stupidity. This is seen as genuinely offensive. If a driver intends making this sign to someone who has cut in on him while driving in town, he will first scan the road ahead to ensure there is no set of traffic lights in sight.

Manners and Etiquette

The Icelanders do not feel themselves bound by the conventions of polite society. They do not go in for formalities such as 'Good morning. How are you?'

The typical Icelander is quiet and restrained. In any meeting he is the man who says nothing and is constantly amazed by those who ask questions. Special amazement is reserved for people who, like the Americans, are able to talk at length on a particular subject. By contrast the Icelander has difficulty in filling five minutes, even if he is a world authority.

To see the Icelander at home, go to the Prikið café in Reykjavik. Here the men of Iceland come early, long before any of the shops have opened, to drink coffee. They sit in gloomy silence, their noses thrust deep into newspapers. Should anyone utter a sound he will receive the withering stares usually reserved for those who sneeze in a library. The men are either blond or bearded. In one corner sits an old man with a deerstalker hat and a stiff moustache. He reads *Morgunbladið*, the national daily, and sips coffee with an air of suspicion. Sit there all day and you will never see him leave. But if you should take your eyes off him for a moment you will notice, when you look again, that he has been replaced by another, almost identical, man.

This public restraint is not matched by private diffidence.

On a one-to-one basis the Icelander is talkative, the high esteem in which he holds himself breaking through the shyness. He will assume you wish to know his opinion about anything and everything. The fact that his opinion may well be irrelevant to your circumstances, or the matter in hand, will be of little importance to him. He is an Icelander, you are an audience (however small), so you will be told.

The Familiar Icelander

Most Icelanders, especially in the towns, have some relationship or other to all the others. They are related, or related by marriage, or they are workmates, ex-school mates or ex-college mates. This means that a quiet morning's shopping can turn into an epic journey through your past life. Just stopping to say hello to such people can turn a quick trip into one requiring three days' leave from work.

To control time loss, elaborate rules of engagement exist. Ex-schoolmates who have not been seen for several years are ignored unless they were particular friends who have moved from the area. A wave will suffice for ex-workmates. For those seen frequently, the standard handshake is used. The Icelanders used to be a more tactile race, the kissing of friends and relatives being the norm, but this gradually came to be seen as altogether too familiar and stopped. However, the French habit of almost kissing both cheeks is now becoming fashionable and has re-awakened the Icelandic enthusiasm for touching.

For distant relatives a handshake, friendly but not too warm, and an enquiry about an old aunt are enough, though a hug might be required if they are rich. A hug and a coffee is much better if they are both rich and old.

The Icelander Overseas

The Icelander abroad will behave in one of two ways, or sometimes both, within the space of an hour. He can be an ambassador for his country (which is not unlikely since he is probably the only Icelander in the area), and he will clean his hotel room before the maid arrives just in case she gets the idea that Icelanders are dirty or untidy. But he can also be aggressive and demanding, even boorish.

Icelanders are amazed and upset to find out that most foreigners neither know nor care where Iceland is. Proud of their linguistic skills, at home they will speak English to visitors at all times, but as soon as they arrive in another country they insist on speaking Icelandic. With little chance of being understood, they can be as insulting as they wish without giving the slightest offence.

Sense of Humour

A man was driving in the wilds of Iceland when his car suddenly stopped. He was not much of a mechanic, but in desperation he lifted up the bonnet and peered at the engine. He was shaking his head in exasperation when a voice beside him said, "It's your carburettor." Turning he found himself face to face with a horse. He fled in horror, running over the brow of a nearby hill. Below he saw a farm and hurtled down to it. He banged on the door and the farmer let him in. He poured out the story to the farmer who sat impassively. When he had finished the farmer said, "What colour was the horse?" The man, stunned by the question, replied "Brown". "Ah," said the farmer, "take no notice of him. That one knows nothing about cars."

This is an unusual Icelandic joke in that almost everybody can appreciate it.

Icelandic humour is an acquired taste, one not normally shared by foreigners. For instance, the whole island rocked with laughter over the tale of an Icelandic woman who married a Turk. When the marriage failed a long legal battle ensued which ended with the man taking their children off to Turkey. To gain revenge the woman ate turkey for Christmas. It can only be assumed that the joke is in the telling, or that the endless dark nights of winter do something to the brain cells.

It was long held that the Icelanders had no sense of humour at all. The grim-faced expression that is the norm (a set born of facing into the winter wind) rarely cracked into a smile. But the Icelanders do have their own humour. It is derived from odd people and odd situations, and relies heavily on word play and spontaneity. In that sense it is similar to British humour, with puns and spoonerisms featuring strongly. A fine example of this is the description of two farms in the north of the country. For reasons lost in time one is called Grave. The other is called On the Edge of the Grave.

Stories about odd people are gentle. In the Westmann Islands a man named Gwilian, who died in 1994 at the age of 81, was known as the The Wanderer right up until his death because in 1927 he had spent 9 months in Reykjavik.

Yet despite the kindness of much of the humour, the Icelanders do have two groups of unfortunates whom they make the butt of 'cruel' humour.

They tell jokes about the overly healthy Norwegians and their passion for sport. But mostly they joke about the inhabitants of Hafnarfjörður, a town a few miles from Reykjavik. In Hafnarfjörður the dustcarts do 100 m.p.h. in case they are robbed, the children take ladders when they start at high school, while their parents take the same ladders shopping if they hear that prices are higher this week. In Icelandic, if the pavements are slippery they are said to be covered in flying ice. If the weather forecast predicts flying ice, Hafnies (people from Hafnarfjörður) sit outside in the cold all night, their eyes glued to the heavens for fear of missing this strange spectacle.

But the tone of the humour is such that the Hafnies tell the jokes too, and have even turned them to their advantage. A Friends of Hafnarfjörður Society has been formed to promote the tall stories and so gain commercial advantage, and the best Hafnie jokes are now told by Hafnies themselves.

Culture

The Sagas

The great Icelandic Sagas were written in the 12th, 13th and early 14th centuries and have been nourishing Icelandic culture constantly ever since. Many ask in all seriousness whether there would have been an Iceland without the Sagas, such a powerful peg are they on which to hang nationhood. The Icelanders are very proud that it was their Viking ancestors who produced these works, there being no equivalent from Denmark, Norway or

Sweden. It is, however, a myth that today's Icelander can read the original texts without transcription.

As a result of constant re-evaluation, the Sagas are as alive now as they were when they were written. Every day on prime time radio (6-6.30 p.m.) there is a fifteen minute reading from one of the Sagas followed by a fifteen minute discussion on the issues the passage raises.

Of such importance are they to the national culture they form the basis of many a modern tale. Among the best of these is that of a truculent taxi driver who was stopped by four students on their way to a celebratory evening. Aware that he was the only car for miles, he decided to make sure that the students were worthy of his services. He said he would not take them unless they were able to quote accurately the first line of *Njal's Saga*. One of the students could and so he happily transported them. It is difficult to think of another European country in which a taxi driver could set such a puzzle or a student answer it.

Books

An Icelandic saying claims that it is better to go barefoot than without books.

More books are published in Iceland per head of population than in any other country and they are of the highest quality. Although prices are outlandish, they sell in large quantities. So while it is said that if you offer a book to an Englishman for Christmas he will say "No thanks, I've got one", an Icelander will be thrilled at the prospect and spend the afternoon going through the shelves of all the local bookshops.

Another Icelandic saying states that if there is a topic in life then there is a book on it. To discover if it is true, all

Icelanders write, some of them profusely. Indeed, writing is a national pastime. The favourite medium is poetry, sometimes in the scaldic metre, a rhythm unique to Iceland largely because no-one else cares enough to use it.

Hér hefur jökullinn	Here the glacier
numið staðar	stopped
á leið sinni	on its path
til sjávar	to the sea
skyggnzt um	looked around
og hlaðið sandvörður	and built sand cairns
	by the roadside

One aspect of the scaldic poem is its use of metaphor, the more complicated, and therefore unintelligible, the better. Thus no *skald* (the term used for a scaldic poet) would dream of calling the sky the sky, not when he could call it 'the hero's hall', or men men, when they could be 'the food of wolves'. The favourite themes are the retelling of the great epics, and lyrical passages on the beauty of the sun going down over the fish-drying frames on cold, misty days in autumn. There is a rumour that Reykjavik is soon to be adorned by a new statue, raised in memory of the lone Icelander who never wrote a poem.

Music

There are fine Icelandic composers, such as Jón Leifs and Arne Björnsson, and their music is played by the National Orchestra.

The fact that Iceland has a National Orchestra is remarkable, not only because so small a country can afford to maintain one, but because enough people can be found to fill it.

Obsessions

Politics and, in particular, the failings of politicians are a national obsession. But the chief obsession is:

The Weather

Icelanders are fond of saying that Iceland does not get real weather, just samples. They also say that if you don't like the weather you just have to wait five minutes and it will change.

What they really mean is that since the island is sandwiched between cold, Arctic air heading south, and warm Gulf Stream air flowing north, it is prone to rapid change. It is possible to experience all four seasons in one day – the speed of the change depending on the strength of the wind. Since the wind usually blows hard, a day that starts out badly, with rain and thick cloud, may be fine by midday. The Icelanders want the visitor to take heart from this. The problem is that if the weather is nice, all you have to do is wait five minutes and then it isn't.

Iceland is close enough to the Arctic Circle to enjoy the midnight sun for several weeks in June and July. It is also close enough to enjoy several weeks in December and January when it does not get light at all. In fact, winters are endured rather than enjoyed. Icelanders like the first snow because it heralds a white Christmas, but by February are sick of it and by April very sick of it indeed. Spring never seems to come, and by the time it has finally arrived, autumn seems just around the corner.

Town dwellers mistreat the snow. It is beaten, gritted, and generally abused and ends up in dirty, sullen heaps at street corners and on the islands in the middle of the road, where it gobbles up the boots of the unwary, making crossing a road as hazardous as any expedition to the Pole.

Then, just when the snow seems beaten, the weather warms suddenly and the heaps melt. Night falls, the temperature drops, and the whole wet mess freezes, so that morning brings a pantomime of slipping people and sliding cars. Sometimes this sequence is repeated for a week or more, by the end of which everyone is short-tempered and near-suicidal.

Knitting

Thirty years ago knitting would have rated a score as high on the national obsession scale as politics and the weather. In country areas it still does, but the town dwellers have long since stopped indulging in this yokel's pursuit, in public at least. Many of Iceland's excellent young artists are women who have put down their knitting needles and taken up paint brushes.

Both men and women knitted. They made triangles for blankets, gloves with fingers but without seams (a skill which still attracts the admiration of the knowledgeable), sweaters, anything to keep out winter's chills. Stories of obsessional knitting are legion. Cow and sheep herders are said to have knitted as they walked across Iceland's rugged landscape. It was even said that farmers' wives knitted while they made love.

The Other Obsession

The other obsession is never mentioned. Icelanders are terrified of toilet rolls, fearing that the ownership of one might imply that the owner is less than perfect.

Before there were supermarkets in Iceland, toilet rolls were wrapped in anonymous brown paper and dropped discreetly out of sight into large shopping bags. Supermarkets have forced people to come clean, in a manner of speaking, though the obsessive fear lives on.

Leisure and Pleasure

The most pleasurable thing the Icelanders can do is spend money, especially if they haven't got any. Perhaps surprisingly, gambling does not appeal to them. (This is fortunate because, apart from the state lottery, it is illegal.) And there are many other things to spend money on.

Holidays

Given the fact that in Iceland bathing in the sea brings on hypothermia in seconds and sunbathing is likely to produce acres of gooseflesh long, long before it produces a tan, it is no surprise that the Icelanders dream of holidays in Spain and Florida. Until a few years ago foreign travel was difficult. The novelty of going abroad has not yet had time to wear off.

Summer Weekend Huts

All town-dwelling Icelanders have timber-built huts out in the middle of nowhere a couple of hours from town. The idea is to use them during spring and summer to escape the rigours of urban living, to rediscover their Icelandic roots, and to be at one with nature.

However, as the town-dwelling Icelander lives in town precisely to avoid the rigours of the country that so plagued his grandfather and father, the huts are rarely visited. They are maintained solely to impress the neighbours.

Driving

The Icelanders drive to such an extent that driving can be considered a leisure activity. Young Icelanders mix this dubious pleasure with that of drinking Coca-Cola, one hand on the steering wheel, the other holding aloft a can or bottle.

Icelanders drive all winter long, for in spite of its name only 11% of the land is covered by permanent glaciers, and the winters are harsh only in the remote centre of the country. No-one could live in the hostile interior, a place so lunar-like that NASA took its astronauts there to train for landing on the moon.

On the coast, where everyone lives, the temperature rarely stays below freezing for very long, and snowfalls, although regular, are more of a nuisance than a hazard. Most drivers carry a spade in the boot as a precaution, and if they do not have a four-wheel drive vehicle, studded tyres, though not compulsory, are absolutely essential.

Four-wheel drive vehicles being a modern invention, all Icelanders must have one, so the roads are frequented by these huge machines fitted with massive wheels which threaten to drive over the top of any ordinary car daft enough to get in the way – like something straight out of *Terminator* 2. In winter they will often be seen dragging horseboxes or vast trailers. These are for snow scooters, which a number of people delight in hauling out of town to some lonely spot, unloading with great effort and then driving aimlessly for an hour or so – just for the thrill of making tracks in the snow.

For some, even this thrill is inadequate, and there are those who fit even bigger wheels and tyres and drive off-road (although in view of the state of the roads this is something of a moot point) tackling snowfields, mountains and glaciers. This form of entertainment was invented by an Icelander, which is just as likely to be due to the fact that no other country could come up with anyone crazy enough to do it, as to the qualities of the northern intellect. Icelanders have driven to places most people do not want to visit.

Infatuation with 'hi-tech' does not end with the vehicle itself. Inside there will be a telephone and a fax machine, a television and a CB radio. There is also likely to be a satellite navigation set. This is particularly handy if the vehicle happens to disappear into a glacial crevasse. The set, being accurate to just a few metres, will be able to tell the occupants almost precisely where they died.

Winter Sport

It is a myth that the Icelander is a hearty outdoor type who finds his country a rugged arena for pursuits which require large boots and a beard. When the snow scooter and glacier-driving fans have departed, the hardy few left outside are foreign skiers.

Most Icelanders stay at home during the winter, peering out anxiously every morning to see if spring has arrived, or else do the sensible thing and go to Spain.

Summer Sport

The Icelanders will try their hand at anything. The newer the sport the better they like it, and if it requires a large amount of expensive equipment they like it even more.

Sport for children is well organised, and individuals do well. Several Icelanders play professional football in Germany and Scandinavia. In team games Iceland does about as well on the world stage as any medium-sized town would expect to do, though they do excel at handball.

The national sport is *glima*, a form of wrestling. Glima is unique to Iceland, though it has similarities to the wrestling practised in Western Samoa. No clear link has been established, and it does seem a long way to go for practice. The sport is very old and involves the wearing of traditional belts and much dancing about before the action starts. It is so popular it never appears on television.

Nightlife

The Icelanders are great ones for entertainment. Centuries of making their own amusement in turf huts during the long dark winters have left them in chronic need of company. As a result there is a huge number of things to do and places to go in the towns – theatres, clubs for all kinds of music, discos, restaurants.

For the committed drinker the weekend starts on Friday afternoon at home. It starts there because it is cheaper to drink at home than in a bar. The rule, therefore, is to drink heavily at home, going out just to finish the job off in the company of a few like-minded people.

For the rest of the population the weekend starts at

midnight, none of the clubs closing before 3 a.m., when everybody moves on to a party.

Dancing was outlawed by the Danes who believed that the high level of illegitimate births in Iceland was attributable to it. After Home Rule had been established, the ban was lifted, since the Icelanders, being a more intelligent people, had worked out that dancing was not the cause.

Cinema

Measured against the population there are four times as many cinemas in a big Icelandic town as there are in other countries.

The Icelanders like the cinema, but not only for the films, which are mainly American or English and have sub-titles rather than being dubbed. Most of the audience follow the dialogue, but use the sub-titles to help out, which means they do not have to catch every spoken word. This is an advantage because the other reason for going to the cinema is to consume vast quantities of pop-corn and to drink huge vats of Coca-Cola. As soon as the film starts, so does the noise, created by hundreds of munching jaws and the crackling of corn, followed by the slurping of hundreds of straws.

After about 45 minutes, right in the middle of a critical scene, the film stops and the lights go up. The consequence of the drinking is now apparent: the audience rise as one and flock out. Ten minutes later everyone reappears, re-supplied with large containers, and the whole procedure starts again.

Old Time Entertainment

A famous old Icelandic book of games for all the family includes one that involved lying people down on their backs, putting a coin on their nose, and laughing at the faces they pulled as they tried to flick the coin off without using their hands. Another game was a race between two groups of four people who passed eggs to one another using spoons held in the mouth. No hands were allowed and the eggs were real. No wonder Icelanders were grateful when television arrived.

Television

American television was available at an early stage of broadcasting history in Iceland. The Icelanders were appalled by the crassness of the advertisements, and since none of the advertised goods was actually for sale in Iceland, they were also able to reinforce their cultural snobbery by noting frequently and at length that they were far too intelligent to be hoodwinked by such rubbish.

However, when the single Icelandic television channel offered advertisements, one company used the saturation technique to sell a foot massager. It was allegedly both useless and unnecessary, but by the end of the campaign it is estimated that 50% of Icelandic houses had one and that no-one had used it more than once.

The most popular television show is a mixture of candid camera situations, *Opportunity Knocks*, chat show, and pantomime. Due to the small size of the population almost every Icelander will appear on the show at some time. Why else would people watch?

Eating and Drinking

The Icelanders are conservative eaters.

As most of their food has to be imported, they have picked up Western habits and tastes. Breakfast is as likely to be cereal and coffee in Iceland as it is in Britain or continental Europe, but older Icelanders do still eat more traditional foods. For breakfast they will have *súrmjólk*, a form of sour milk, which looks and tastes like thin, light yogurt; or *Rist með Osti*, hot toast served with butter, marmalade and thinly-sliced cheese. (Iceland does not permit the importation of cheese, but as Icelanders like the taste of certain foreign cheeses, such as Stilton and Brie, they produce their own versions.)

For that important mid-morning snack to keep hunger pangs at bay, the kiosks at bus stations and most bakeries sell rolls of exaggerated length and dubious content and cakes shaped like prehistoric ammonites. These huge buns are topped with sugar or a type of icing which is coloured either pink or dark brown.

Lunch is a sandwich or something equally light. The main meal of the day is eaten in the evening and for this fish and lamb are the favourites. Smoked lamb (*saltkjöt*) which has been hung over a lamb-dung fire is as close to the real flavour of the country as it is possible to get – it is said that the fire must be lamb dung to give the taste an extra piquancy. This may well be true. What is definitely true is that Icelandic lamb, smoked or not, is delicious. Unusual fish dishes, such as cod cheeks, are tender and full of flavour. Fresh vegetables and fruit are shipped in all year round, and some vegetables, such as carrots, potatoes and cauliflowers, are home-grown.

Although there is a limited range of Icelandic dishes, there are traditional Viking delicacies, which are claimed to be both original and very popular. One such is rams' testicles pickled in whey. Others include congealed blood pudding, shark meat putrefied by being buried in the ground for several months, seal flipper soured in a way best left undefined, and boiled and pressed sheep's head.

Icelanders are surprised that the only authentic Viking restaurant in Reykjavik is not popular with visitors. Visitors do not share this surprise. Indeed, they wonder at the existence of even one Viking restaurant.

Another Viking speciality can be found on the Westmann Islands, off the southern coast. During the spring nesting season, the islanders collect puffins and puffin eggs. To do this they throw themselves off the cliffs attached to thin ropes, and as they swing about, hundreds of feet above the lashing sea, they collect the eggs. Adult birds are netted on the cliff tops, an equally dangerous activity. Despite these antics having most clearly had their origins in starvation, the youth of the islands now practice the tradition as a sport, seeing who can travel the furthest, perform the most elegant arc, and survive.

Considering how close the collectors come to killing themselves, you would assume that puffin tastes like ambrosia. You would be mistaken. Pan-fried, boiled, braised or roasted – nothing can make the bird taste like anything other than used sump oil.

Puffin is not as popular as dried fish. All over Iceland, but particularly in the north, fish of all types are hung out to dry on huge fish-drying frames like clothes on a line. They are left until they are as thin as paper and taste of old carpet. When the seagulls have lost interest in the fish the Icelanders will soon consider them ready to eat.

Eating out is a favourite pastime, though it must be said that it is a very expensive one. As in all cosmopolitan capital cities, it is possible to eat in any style in Reykjavik – Italian, Indian, Chinese. There is even a 'One Woman

Vegetarian' restaurant.

One of the most fashionable restaurants is the Pearl. It sits on top of a giant hot water tank, built to store volcanically-heated water for the central heating systems of the city. The restaurant revolves, adding an extra dimension – indeed, several – to a meal. This is ludicrous or brilliant fun, depending upon your point of view, but since it is too expensive to eat there, it doesn't really make any difference one way or the other.

Coffee

The traditional drink in Icelandic cafés is coffee, not tea. The coffee varies from drinkable to lethal. Icelanders thrive on it, but visitors, especially those of a more delicate palate, might well find that two cups will bring on the shakes.

Many older Icelanders do not add sugar to their coffee but keep a *sykurmoli* (sugarcube) in their mouths while they are drinking, a habit which could go some way to explaining the silence of coffee drinkers. Although the young are adopting the Western habit of adding sugar, the name lives on in *Sykurmolarnir* – The Sugarcubes – one of the island's most popular rock groups. Björk Guðmundsdóttir, the elfin-like pop singer who won the British award as rock music's best, was the lead singer for this group at one time.

Alcohol

It is said that God's gift to the Icelanders was a virgin land of incomparable beauty and diversity. The price the modern Icelanders have to pay for the gift is the cost of alcohol.

Until 1st March 1989 beer was banned and even now is only available at state-controlled outlets at extortionate prices. The idea that the earlier prohibition would reduce drunkenness flew in the face of both logic and experience. In common with those other Vikings in Norway and Sweden the Icelander long ago sorted out the problem of the long, dark winter months. The solution was straight-forward: get drunk in September and don't sober up until late April.

Under prohibition, alcohol was available at certain times and places, one of which was when you were airborne on an internal flight. The result was that drinking started as the plane was taxi-ing to the end of the runway and stopped only when the doors opened at flight's end. By then it was usually possible to pour the passengers out of the plane rather than have them disembark in the usual way.

Another effect of prohibition was that alcohol smuggling and illicit stills for bootleg drink were common-place. The home-made version was so awful that large quantities of Coca-Cola had to be consumed to drown the taste. Habits die hard, and many older Icelanders still drink copious amounts of Coke, keeping the youth of the country company.

Drinking is now legal, but controlled. Alcohol of any description can only be bought at the government liquor stores and is very expensive. Drinking is permitted in restaurants and bars where it is even more expensive. The effect of making alcohol more accessible has been to reduce the amount consumed, but it has had no effect on the nature of drinking. Icelanders do not understand social drinking. They drink purely to get drunk, a condi-tion they seek with maximum enthusiasm at minimum expense. If it costs 10% less to get drunk on gin than on whisky, they will drink gin. Enquire whether taste is a consideration and they will look at you as though you are stupid. What could taste have to do with it?

As if to prove the point, the only truly Icelandic drink, *brennivin*, which is made from potatoes, tastes of nothing, cuts the throat like liquid emery paper, and is known, with very good reason, as 'black death'.

Since alcohol became legal, smuggling has decreased dramatically. This gladdens the heart of the coastguards, but is mourned by the media. For years the frequent chases and fights between smuggling seamen and officials provided great copy, as well as black eyes and other injuries. But because alcohol is so expensive, home brewing is on the increase, especially among the young, and there are frequent rumours of stills operating again in the wilds of lonely valleys.

1st March is National Beer Day, celebrating the end of prohibition. The festivities take the form of a 24-hour-long binge largely indistinguishable from the celebrations on all other days. It is difficult to imagine what might happen if beer was cheaper – just how do you tell the man who has drunk too much at £4 a pint from the one who has drunk too much at £2 a pint?

Conversation with a drinking Icelander is either impossible or futile, but in the unlikely event of your getting the chance, the Icelandic for 'cheers' is '*skáe*', pronounced scowl.

While you sit with your drink you can contemplate the close shave the government had in naming the Ministry responsible for alcohol – the Alcohol and Tobacco Department (A.T.V.R.). Originally it was to have been called the Tobacco and Alcohol (T.A.R.), but at the last minute someone noticed that this would be pronounced 'tear'. An Icelandic slang expression for drinking is 'to have a tear', and the appalling embarrassment of the name became apparent. It was changed, at some cost.

Custom and Tradition

Names and Patronyms

The majority of Icelandic Christian names come from the Sagas. There you find Harald of the Grey Cape and Bork Blue Tooth Beard. Today it is possible to have a drink with Stone, son of Wolf (Stein Úlfsson), or with Eagle, son of Bear (Einnar Bjornson). And, what is more, it is possible to do so without having your head cleaved in twain and your wife broached.

Icelanders are very proud of being the only Viking country to maintain patronyms, the use of the father's given name as the child's surname. The usage produces the oddity of a standard nuclear family of father, mother, son and daughter having four different surnames. If Petúr, the son of Björn, marries Guðrun, daughter of Vilhjàm, and they have two children, Martha and Einnar, then in a European hotel the family will sign in as Petúr Björnsson, Guðrun Vilhjàmsdóttir, Martha Petúrsdóttir and Einnar Petúrsson. Hotel receptionists have been known to weep.

The use of patronyms has the potential to make the telephone directory one of the most difficult books in the world to follow. To counter the problem, the book lists everybody by both their Christian names and surnames. But this is only a partial solution as there is a limited number of Christian names, so that there are always several people with the same names. The next obvious addition would be the address, but the Icelanders add the profession of the person, and only then is the address given. Almost as if it were an afterthought the telephone number is listed, though by the time they have waded through all the information, most people have forgotten why they wanted to ring anyway.

The Nobel prizewinning author, Halldor Laxness, is one of a very small number of Icelanders who have taken a European-style surname. In others this would be looked down on as an affectation. In his case it is acceptable because he is a genius.

Þorrablót

The earliest Icelanders had a miserable time during the five months of winter, even more miserable than their modern compatriots.

To keep themselves sane they held regular festivals. Midwinter was enthusiastically celebrated, and still is, although it is now called Christmas, but one of the main festivals was *þorrablót*, held during the third week of January. *Þorri* was the fourth month of winter. When it was over (by the third week of February), only the last weeks of winter remained, the days were getting longer rapidly and spring was on the way.

The festival of þorri involved a week of feasting. It also became traditional for Icelanders to welcome þorri by putting only one leg into their trousers and hopping around the yard barefoot. The church tried to end the festival (not least, perhaps, to avoid half the congregation hobbling in on crutches as a result of a single frost-bitten foot), but it was revived under Danish rule as a symbol of nationalism.

Today it is enthusiastically celebrated for much the same reasons that the earliest settlers enjoyed it. Traditional foods are eaten and much drink is consumed. Bare-legged hopping is no longer compulsory, but is likely to occur at those gatherings where sufficient lubrication has been provided to remove all inhibitions.

Ash Wednesday

In a festival that still mixes the pagan past and the Christian present, on Ash Wednesday all Icelandic children put on fancy dress and spend the day trying to humiliate adults.

Quite the weirdest aspect of the festival is *kattarslagur* in which the children use home-made swords or clubs to sever a rope suspended through a barrel. Not so long ago, for reasons lost in the mists of time, a dead cat was hung on the end of the rope. Nowadays, to the relief of all concerned, and most especially the Icelandic cat population, a fluffy toy hangs from the rope.

Ash Wednesday is preceded by Bun Day, the Icelandic equivalent of Shrove Tuesday. This sounds normal enough, but even this Icelandic festival includes the bizarre, the tradition being to receive a bun for having hit someone across the backside with a stick before he/she has got out of bed. In most other countries such activity would more likely result in the perpetrator being rewarded with a big fat fine.

Health and Hygiene

Life and Death

The Icelanders have the highest life expectancy of any country in the world other than people in (the ex-Soviet State of) Georgia who are said to live regularly to 125.

Not very many years ago doctors were in short supply in Iceland. The best that could be obtained in country areas was the district nurse who would probably not be available in spring as she would be busy castrating that year's rams. A wise old family member would be all that was left for consultation. As a result, Icelanders are of the opinion that any ailment or pain is a minor problem, an inconvenience that will right itself in an hour or two, or a day at most.

It comes as a surprise when they die, that being the last thing they expected to happen. Death itself is handled with a minimum of fuss, the chief participant in the event being lowered into the ground with little ceremony.

Unfortunately American television is now putting this healthy aspect of Icelandic life into a proper perspective. The young Icelander is slowly realising that the Americans could well be right and that all minor ailments and pains are quite likely to be bubonic plague. Potions and pills are catching on.

Death, too, is becoming big business, people having realised that their funerals are the last available status symbol. Increasingly, bands are being hired to play the favourite music of the deceased, and parties organised. Absolved of all responsibility for the actions of the guests and the expense of it all, the corpses have the time of their lives.

Health Service

The Icelanders claim that their high life expectancy is due in part to their excellent national health service. They pay just a small fee when they go to a doctor, a bigger one to see a specialist.

The health service does not extend to dentists which is not surprising, considering the quantity of sweets consumed by Icelanders of all ages. There is no insurance cover available for dentistry either. It is quite simple: you eat sweets, you get bad teeth, you go to the dentist and afterwards you settle his bill. The pain might be in your mouth, but you will certainly pay through the nose. The redeeming feature of this financial consideration is that it has promoted good oral hygiene, so that despite all the sugar in their diet the Icelanders are rarely obliged to pay for fillings.

Condoms

Never having suffered from the puritanism of the Saxons, Icelanders fix their condom selling machines on the walls of bus stations rather than hiding them away in the 'Gents'. Even this has not been enough to prevent Aids obtaining a toe-hold. The latest attempt to reduce the spread of the disease has been the decision to sell condoms in taxis. This is a sensible measure, though Icelanders live in fear of the taxi driver demanding that they recite the first lines of *Njal's Saga* before he will part with a packet.

Hygiene

Icelanders are both healthy and hygienic. The former they put down to the latter. All towns have open-air swimming pools where all the year round Icelanders swim daily, the old folk early, the schoolchildren and parents later in the day.

The water for the pools is volcanically heated so that even in winter, when the road outside is covered in snow and the wind is trying to move the water from the deep end to the shallow end, the Icelanders will still be lapping steadily. It is a strange sight, steam from the hot water adding a surreal touch to the sight of heads covered with frost bobbing relentlessly up and down.

Beside the pools are circular hot pots into which steps descend. The railings around them vary in colour from pink to bright red. These colours match those of the skins of the occupants, the volcanic water in them varying from hot in the first pot to unbelievably hot in the last. The Icelanders rest in these prior to, and after, swimming. They do not view the colour of the pot as some form of virility symbol, but most visitors do. Stories are legion of visitors hurling themselves into the hottest pot and exiting seconds later with eyes bulging and strangulated screams.

Before swimming, it is compulsory to shower and wash. Free soap and shampoo are supplied and the volcanic shower water can be as hot as you can bear. Anyone attempting to enter the pool without showering will be met with the wrath of the attendant. The men's side and the women's side employ an identical version: small and thin, but caustic of tongue and armed with a broom.

With all this showering and swimming the Icelanders are very clean. The only slight drawback is that the volcanic water stinks of sulphur. It takes a while for outsiders to get used to the idea that very clean people can stink of rotten eggs.

Government and Bureaucracy

Politics

The Icelanders are very proud of having been the first nation in the world to have elected a woman as head of state. President Vigdis Finnbogadóttir has been persuaded to stay on for more than one term, but the Icelanders' attitude to her is in marked contrast to that afforded to other politicians.

In general the Icelanders dislike politicians. To a race that views itself as sophisticated and cultured, politics seems a very backward profession to choose, the province of the stupid and corrupt. They hold all politicians in low esteem and every couple of years give them the opportunity of finding a decent way of earning a living by the straightforward expedient of kicking them out.

Having no national rude gesture (though suitable gestures borrowed from other countries via television and films are used with great enthusiasm), the Icelanders have to content themselves with publicly humiliating those they wish to offend. The greatest humiliations are reserved for their politicians, the very greatest for those who attain the highest offices. You can be sure that if a politician has an offensive nickname, he has been singled out for high office. If it is really offensive, he is probably the prime minister.

In keeping with the national trend, the newspapers are vehement and caustic about all politicians; indeed, it is generally assumed that reporters are under an obligation to be insulting. However, the source of their ire is not that politicians are evil or womanisers, but that they are inept and stupid. Affairs of state attract more attention than more everyday affairs, though it is more likely that the latter go unreported than that they do not exist.

By contrast, those who are insulted by politicians are horrified. It is as though the ducks had started to shoot back. A television producer with a string of deeply offensive political shows to his credit was insulted – as he saw it – by a government minister. The cries of outrage were pitiful and he promptly formed the Association of People Who Have Been Insulted By Politicians with the intention of supporting libel cases for those who found themselves in a similar position.

The current Prime Minister is a satirist's dream. He is leader of the Independence Party, the party with the largest number of seats, which holds power in a moderately right-wing coalition with the Social Democrats. He is small and round, and has a mop of curly hair. A recent savage attack suggested that the hair and a certain darkness of the features could be traced to a Caribbean influence. This was emphatically denied, family lines back to the 9th century being offered for public scrutiny.

The whole debate was irrelevant to politics, but was hugely enjoyed, the more so since the PM in his student days had been part of a radio comedy show which specialised in being spiteful to politicians.

Iceland has 63 members of parliament drawn from five main parties one of which is the Women's List. The ten-man coalition cabinet has been rightish of centre for more years than can be remembered, though this seems to matter little to the Icelanders who believe that the differences between a useless right-wing government and a useless left-wing government are frequently overstated in other western countries.

A recent poll suggested that despite a leftward trend in politics there were just three communists in the country. One was the gum-chewing presenter of Iceland's best radio jazz programme. The second was the keeper of the most northerly lighthouse, a man known as Ole the

Commie, who is rumoured to have a picture of Stalin on the lighthouse wall. The third person was not named for fear of libel action.

As the Independence Party has led governments and coalitions since 1904, rumours of corruption, patronage and nepotism are rife. These are widely believed to exist, although there has never been a formal investigation. The Icelanders just accept this situation, together with the somewhat obvious gerrymandering of constituencies that often goes on before elections, with a sigh and a shake of the head. This may go some way towards explaining both the savageness of the satire and the general attitude that it is best to get on with having a good time before the mad buggers in power mess it all up.

Perhaps the last word should go to a politician. A Prime Minister was asked what he thought of the constant stream of abuse to which the people subjected him. He thought for a moment and then said, 'Well, if they don't like me why do they vote for me?' It was a good question, especially as he was voted in again at the next election.

The Civil Service

The Civil Service, having been around for the same length of time as the coalition, looks more like the government than the politicians do and this has led to the suggestion that Iceland could successfully do away with one layer of government, namely the elected layer. The only problem would be that the unelected government, i.e. the Civil Service, takes itself far too seriously.

Even when the government has voted in favour of something, it can sometimes be difficult to get it done.

There will be some junior clerk in some obscure ministry who does not like the idea. Once he has halted progress the whole stubborn machinery of the Civil Service will come in on his side and it will be lost in a welter of red tape. The fact that something is official policy is of no consequence if it does not happen to be Civil Service policy.

Systems

Roads

To drive around Iceland takes days. Visitors to þingvellir, the site of the world's first parliament, will find that the road is good, being metalled all the way. The vast majority of visitors stop at þingvellir and so don't know that beyond the next bend the road reverts to the Icelandic norm. This is a gravel track that frequently degenerates into a gravel track interspersed with pot holes, the dimensions of which have been carefully organised so that they are very slightly bigger than the relevant wheel/suspension size of the largest car. A journey takes on epic proportions as the driver weaves between the holes, desperately searching for a length of road that will not interfere with his digestion.

The only advantage of the condition of the roads is that the Icelanders have never been persuaded to take part in the curse of the metalled road, i.e. the owning and towing of caravans.

Periodically a landslip, caused by summer's rain or winter's snow, will inundate the road. The Icelanders remain unmoved by this, merely calling out a steam roller to flatten the soil heap and then driving over it.

At intervals on the roadside a curious sign will be seen – *blindhaeð*. This means the next section should be driven with care as the road is about to go over a hump. Despite the fact that in this sparsely-populated country it is possible to drive all day without actually getting anywhere or meeting anyone, the hump will always be hiding the one car that is coming in the opposite direction.

To help the poorly-sighted at pedestrian crossings in Reykjavik, a ticking noise has been added to the green 'walk' signal. The noise is all but inaudible, but when it can be heard, the listener usually assumes that one of the small folk has become trapped inside the device and is knocking to be let out. By the time the confusion is over the 'walk' light has changed to red.

By Plane and Bus

Keflavik is probably the most beautiful airport in the world and certainly the only one built on a piece of land obtained 1000 years ago in exchange for an embroidered cloak. In contrast to all other airports, Keflavik sells duty-free goods to incoming as well as outgoing visitors. The Icelanders want your money.

Iceland has an excellent internal air service. The bus system is equally good. Given a few weeks one can travel all the way around the island, stopping off to see things before hopping back on the bus again. It can come as a surprise, though, when on a Monday morning the reply to the question "When is the next bus?" is "Wednesday afternoon". Bus stops are not well equipped for those who decide to wait.

You can't catch a train because there aren't any.

Education

Formal education starts when children are six, though there are plenty of pre-school groups that take children for the day or half-day from three years old. Compulsory schooling lasts from six to sixteen, after which there is high school until the age of twenty.

At this stage many youngsters either go abroad or go on to university. There are two universities, in Reykjavik and Akureyri, but being a small country means that Iceland does not have the resources to cover all subjects. So if you want to study subjects such as architecture or post-graduate medicine you must go abroad, and a staggering number of students do so.

Going abroad has advantages and disadvantages. The advantage of foreign study is that it makes Iceland more cosmopolitan since students tend to talk to each on their return. In the United States two students of the same discipline studying in different parts of Europe might finish up 3,000 miles apart and never hear of each other again. In Iceland, they may well live in adjacent streets and meet up in the supermarket. The disadvantage of overseas travel is that students tend to see their homeland as small and parochial.

The Power System

In spite of having no coal or oil, the Icelanders have an almost perfect power system, being blessed with lashings of hot water. Some water is used to generate electricity, and more is used to provide central heating systems in the houses. The water is metered and paid for by the gallon.

Even the waste water – which is still quite warm – is

utilised, pipes being run under the pavements to melt the winter's snow and ice. This system is not organised by the town councils, so individual householders have to pay for the pipes to be installed. It is therefore possible to walk along a street that has a snow heap that requires mountaineering skills, a section of clean, wet pavement, then a tricky iced section where the pipes don't exist, and then another snow mountain. It pays to be alert.

Emergency Services

There is a coastguard service, a very efficient one, which more or less stands in for army, navy and air force. During the Cod Wars a coastguard boat with a machine gun mounted on the front was a match for the Royal Navy.

The Fire Brigade

Nothing ever seems to burn down during the Icelandic winter, so the fire brigade spends its time making savings for the national health service. This they do by climbing up to the gutterings of high buildings to remove icicles the size of the Sword of Damocles.

In the summer months the brigade deals with a few fires. It cannot fill in its time by rescuing the odd cat stuck up a tree as there are no trees.

Crime and Punishment

The story is told of a group of men enjoying a meal in a Reykjavik restaurant when a drunk, lurching towards the door, stole a coat belonging to one of them. The group pursued him, stopping a passing police car so that he could be arrested. The drunk, the coat and the coat's owner were taken to the police station where the drunk was put in a cell and the coat-owner assisted with the filling out of the necessary forms. That completed, the man asked what would happen to the drunk. "Well," said the policeman in charge, "would you like to go into the cell and knock him about a bit?" "What?" said the man, shocked by the suggestion, "he's twice the size of me". "Hmm,' said the policeman, "you have a point. Would you like us to go in first and mollify him a little?"

Every Icelander would deny this tale of course, though only after they had told it. But it illustrates some basics about Icelandic justice which is rooted in the old Viking idea of natural justice and administered by policemen who are on the side of the injured party.

The Police

The police, who are known as *lagre*, a shortened form of the Icelandic for 'servant of the law', are liked. Little boys want to grow up to be policemen, although this may have something to do with their being unable to grow up to be train drivers. Parents do not object since the police are seen as friendly and by no means the hard hand of the state.

The police are hot on speeding and all police vehicles are fitted with radar speed guns. They are even hotter on drink-driving. The merest suspicion of alcohol in a driver's blood and he is in very hot water indeed.

Crime

When the Russian trawlers dock there is said to be a sharp increase in crime in Iceland. This story is widely believed to be true, but is treated with scorn by many who feel it is propaganda put out by the government to draw attention away from the increasing problems caused by unemployment and drugs.

Most crime is drink-related, the Icelanders being aggressive when they have had too much to drink. Window breaking is very popular, particularly with Iceland's glaziers, as a stroll downtown on a Sunday morning will show. However, the drink and drug users have started breaking heads as well, and this is a different issue. When men who had had too much to drink fought each other that was their affair, but when upstanding citizens start getting hurt it is quite another matter.

Occasionally, there is a death as a result of a drunken brawl and someone is charged with manslaughter. Murder is very unusual, so rare in fact that one murder which took place in the north of the country in the early 19th century still attracts debate.

When another took place in 1990, the lagre called in a detective from Hamburg because they felt so out of their depth. In the nature of finding a way of making cash from virtually any situation, the murderer has written a best-selling book on salmon fishing.

Tax evasion is the serious white-collar crime, costing the state millions every year, but most Icelanders show little concern as the state is seen as fair game. If someone is caught it is felt to be more bad luck than justice.

Business

There is a close association between big business and the leading political party, an association which is seen as too close, especially when the politicians become spokesmen for the businesses, and when the directors of the leading banks (very high earners) are political appointees.

The Icelanders are strong believers in the existence of the *Kol Krabbe* (Octopus), an organisation (probably informal but, as always with these things, who knows?) of the country's fourteen leading families who control the major businesses and have members within the government. The sighting of two of them in a car is usually accompanied by sneering comments about meetings of the Kol Krabbe, though as with all other political scandals the Icelanders much prefer sarcasm and insults to real action.

Weak trades unions have given businessmen the edge in wage negotiations, while centuries of history have bred an independence of mind. This combination means that most Icelanders aspire to be their own bosses, and many set up businesses, starting small and usually getting smaller before they disappear.

If the Taiwanese invent battery-operated back scratchers, you can rest assured that by the end of the first week of production an Icelander will have formed a business to import them. Money will be borrowed, premises hired and staff employed but, more often than not, to no avail, the bottom falling out of the back scratcher market within two weeks.

One might imagine that the Icelanders, being an intelligent race, would learn from their mistakes. But their faith in economists and their own abilities is without limits.

The Government approves of all this commerce, one minister having been tempted to state that the number of bankruptcies in the country was a measure of its economic health. This is an interesting view and one that would certainly be appreciated by the importer of several thousand back scratchers.

The exceptions to the rules of Icelandic economics are the fishermen. They are the highest-paid workers in the country, earning five times the salary of a university lecturer. They have tax concessions as well, and a recent attempt by the government to reduce these was followed by a fishermen's march to the parliament building. Such direct action was so unusual and shocking that the government backed down immediately.

Language and Ideas

The Dane, Rasmus Christian Rask, claimed in the early 19th century that he had learned Icelandic in order to be able to think. This was a wonderful, even moving, compliment. But he also predicted that Icelandic would be dead in 100 years, killed off by Danish, the language of the island's rulers. Danish was the language of commerce and government. It was also the language of snobbery, used by the Icelandic 'gentry'. It is ironical that the Icelanders' dislike of pretension and the working man's dislike of the upper class saved the language from extinction. Similar predictions are now being made about the death of Icelandic at the hands of English. These are also likely to be an exaggeration.

To the list of obsessions another could have been added – Icelandic. Icelandic is an exotic language based on an alphabet with 33 letters, the extra ones being extremely picturesque and completely unpronounceable.

A poem in Icelandic by William Holm expresses it thus:

'In an airconditioned room you cannot understand the
    grammar of this language,
The whirring machine drowns out the soft vowels,
But you can hear these vowels in the mountain wind
And in heavy seas breaking over the hull of a small boat.
Old ladies can wind their long hair in this language
And can hum, and knit, and make pancakes.
But you cannot have a cocktail party in this language
And say witty things standing up with a drink in your hand.
You must sit down to speak this language,
It is so heavy you can't be polite or chatter in it.
For once you have begun a sentence, the whole course of
    your life is laid out before you,
Every foolish mistake is clear, every failure, every grief,
Moving around the inflections from case to case and gender
    to gender,
The vowels changing and darkening, the consonants softening
    on the tongue
Till they are the sound of a gull's wings fluttering
As he flies out of the wake of a small boat drifting out to
    open water.'

The Icelanders are as proud of their language as they
are of their country and protect it fiercely from external
invasion. Committees set up to protect the language go to
great lengths to avoid absorbing foreign words. When a
new concept or invention is imported into Iceland, the
relevant committee sets about the production of an
Icelandic equivalent. The Sagas are scoured for a word no
longer in common usage that can be pressed into service.
To avoid 'telephone' the word *simi* was dredged up, an
ancient word for a thread. 'Satellite' presented a problem,
but *geryitungl* was manufactured from the words for

'artificial' and 'moon'. Television is called *sjonvarp*, combining the words for seeing and casting out (as in fishing).

Very occasionally something comes along that creates a real problem: what to do, for instance, with 'intercontinental ballistic missile'? The Sagas did not offer a word for 'spear thrown from a great distance' so a new one had to be concocted which means 'long distance fiery flying thing'. It is no surprise that most Icelanders say ICBM.

No Icelandic words inhabit the international household, though the Icelanders do lay claim to several of Viking origin that have found their way into English. Best of all they like *berserk*, probably deriving from 'bear-skin' and used as a term for warriors who fought with the strength of ten men and were immune to pain. It is likely that berserkers were totally intoxicated, a condition much favoured by the population.

The Icelanders are pleased to the point of embarrassment if a foreigner learns their language. In 1993 it was discovered that a Georgian lawyer had taught himself Icelandic. He did not know any Icelanders and had done it purely for his own enjoyment, translating a quantity of Icelandic literature into his own language. The Icelanders were both impressed and grateful. They invited the man and his wife to Iceland at the country's expense, and wined and dined them for two months.

The Author

Richard Sale was born in England's West Country – reason enough to feel sympathy with all minorities who speak with strange tongues.

Being quite good at sums, he took a degree in theoretical physics and a Ph.D. in astrophysics, and then sought a job in glaciology in order to be nearer to his first great loves – snow and ice. He is now a travel writer, specialising in wilderness areas, most particularly the Arctic.

He fell in love with Iceland the first time he saw it – barely, through the fine rain that was falling – and has been going there, summer and winter, ever since. He is endlessly fascinated by its mixture of landscapes, its birdlife and its people (though not always in that order), and constantly frustrated by its weather.

He would like to thank several Icelandic friends for their (sometimes inadvertent) assistance with this book. Sadly, none of them is willing to be identified.

He has received a great deal of help from his Arctic travel colleague, Tony Oliver, who was also once a physicist but graduated to greater things, like making bicycles and taking photographs for a living.

On joint Icelandic expeditions they have spent many freezing winter nights huddled in tents, and are convinced they have only survived the experience because in Britain they live 300 miles apart.